WAR FOR INDEPENDENCE

THE
AMERICAN
REVOLUTION

Rebellious farmers fight veteran British soldiers at
Concord Bridge on the first day of the American Revolution.

WAR FOR INDEPENDENCE

THE

AMERICAN REVOLUTION

ALDEN R. CARTER

FRANKLIN WATTS
A Division of Grolier Publishing
New York London Hong Kong Sydney
Danbury, Connecticut

ACKNOWLEDGMENTS

Many thanks to all who helped with *The American Revolution: War for Independence*, particularly my editors, Reni Roxas and Lorna Greenberg; my mother, Hilda Carter Fletcher; and my friends Barbara Feinberg and Dean Markwardt. As always, my wife, Carol, deserves much of the credit.

This book is for my daughter, Siri.

Cover: The Battle of Princeton, January 3, 1777.
Maps by Bill Clipson
Cover photograph copyright © The Historical Society of Pennsylvania
Photographs copyright ©: The Olde Print Shop: pp. 2, 16 bottom, 21, 56; North Wind Picture Archives, Alfred, ME.: pp. 10, 18, 27, 29 top, 40, 42, 51, 55; The Bettmann Archive: p. 12; Historical Pictures Service, Chicago: pp. 14, 43; The Paul Revere Life Insurance Co., Worcester, MA.: p. 16 top; New York Public Library, Picture Collection: pp. 23, 25, 29 bottom, 31, 36, 38, 47; Fort Ticonderoga Museum: p. 35; West Point Museum Collection: p. 59.

Library of Congress Cataloging-in-Publication Data

Carter, Alden R.
The American Revolution : war for independence / Alden R. Carter.
p.   cm.—(A First book)
Includes bibliographical references and index.
Summary: Discusses the causes, events, campaigns, personalities, and aftermath of the American revolutionary war.
ISBN 0-531-20082-5 (lib. bdg.) / ISBN 0-531-15652-4 (pbk.)
1. United States—History—Revolution, 1775–1783—Juvenile literature.   [1. United States—History—Revolution, 1775–1783.]
I. Title.   II. Series.
E208.C327   1992
973.3—dc20   92-5586 CIP AC

FRANKLIN WATTS
A Division of Grolier Publishing
Sherman Turnpike
Danbury, CT 06813

CONTENTS

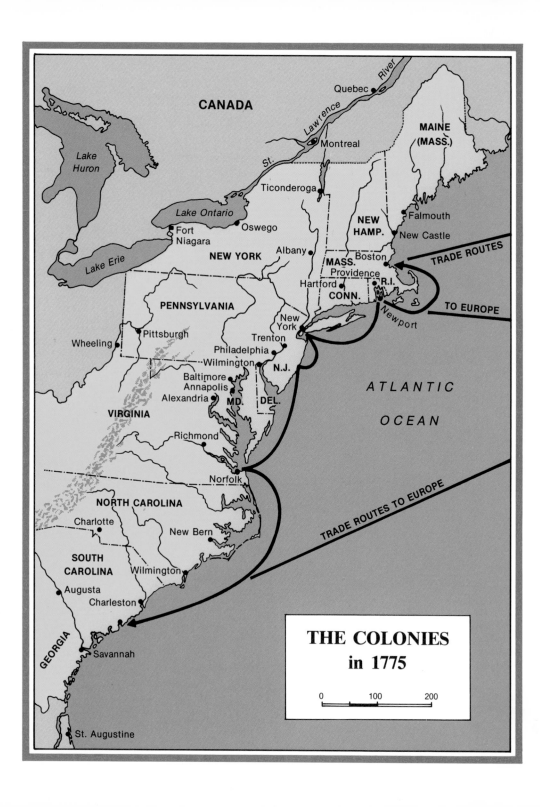

CANADA

Quebec

Lawrence River

MAINE
(MASS.)

Lake
Huron

St.

Montreal

Lake Ontario

Ticonderoga

Oswego

Falmouth

NEW
HAMP.

New Castle

Fort
Niagara

Albany

Boston

TRADE ROUTES

Lake Erie

NEW YORK

MASS.

Providence

Hartford

R.I.

TO EUROPE

PENNSYLVANIA

CONN.

Newport

New
York

ATLANTIC

Pittsburgh

Trenton

Wheeling

Philadelphia

OCEAN

Wilmington

N.J.

Baltimore

Annapolis

Alexandria

MD.

DEL.

VIRGINIA

Richmond

Norfolk

TRADE ROUTES TO EUROPE

NORTH CAROLINA

Charlotte

New Bern

SOUTH
CAROLINA

Wilmington

Augusta

Charleston

GEORGIA

Savannah

THE COLONIES
in 1775

0   100   200

St. Augustine

ONE

THE SHOT HEARD ROUND THE WORLD

T H E   D E W lay heavy on the village green of Lexington, Massachusetts, in the predawn chill of April 19, 1775. A crowd of about seventy farmers and villagers stood shivering around the open door of Buckman's Tavern. They talked in low, anxious voices, their fingers fidgeting on muskets grabbed from walls and corners at the call to arms. It had been a night of alarms, of breathless neighbors hammering on the doors of darkened homes, of galloping hoofbeats and shouted warnings in the dark, of booming signal guns and ringing church bells in villages down the road toward Boston. The British were coming—marching into the countryside to stamp out the spirit of rebellion in King George III's unruly colony.

Many years of argument had brought Britain and America to this explosive moment. The first English colonists had come to North America in the early 1600s in search of religious, personal, and economic freedom. With great toil, they had established thriving colonies in Virginia and Massachusetts. Their success inspired many thousands to quit Europe for the opportunities of the New World. Thirteen colonies grew up along the Atlantic seaboard from Maine (then part of Massachusetts) to Georgia. The colonies were largely self-governing. The British king appointed or approved governors, but assemblies elected by the colonists made laws, set taxes, and raised companies of troops, called militia, to defend the colonies.

As the colonies grew, they pushed the Native Americans westward and began entering lands claimed by the French settlers of Canada. The French and Indians fought back in four wars, beginning in 1689 and lasting on and off for nearly seventy-five years. Britain occasionally sent warships and small numbers of soldiers to America, but large British armies did not arrive until 1755. British victory in the French and Indian War (called the Seven Years' War in Europe) drove the French from North America and made Britain into a great empire with colonies on nearly every continent. With the threat of the French gone, the American colonists expected even more freedom as they expanded trade with the outside world and settled the lands west of the Appalachian Mountains. Britain, however, decided that the colonies should give up some of their independent ways to help pay the cost of running the empire.

The king shared power with the British legislature, the Parliament. From its ranks he chose a prime minister to run the government. Few members of Parliament knew much about America, and the colonies had no vote in its decisions. In 1763, Parliament began passing laws to bring tighter control over the colonies. It closed the western lands to settlement and revised the taxes, called duties, on colonial trade. The government dispatched soldiers, war-ships, and a small army of tax collectors to enforce the new rules. Deaf to loud American protests, Parliament next passed a law requiring a tax stamp on all legal documents written in the colonies. The Stamp Act was Parliament's first try at taxing business *within* the colonies—a right jealously guarded by the colonial assemblies.

The law brought a summer of marches and riots called the Stamp Act Crisis of 1765. Patriots organized to fight for American rights, establishing ties with groups in other colonies through "committees of correspondence." In Boston, the firebrand Samuel Adams (1722–1803) led the Sons of Liberty in a boycott of the buying and selling of British goods. The boycott spread through the colonies, cutting trade with Britain to a trickle. Meanwhile, nine colonial assemblies sent delegates to New York City for the Stamp Act Congress. They agreed that since Parliament contained no American representatives, it had no right to tax the colonies. "No taxation without representation" became the colonial motto.

British business owners hurt by the boycott forced repeal of the Stamp Act, but Parliament soon outraged the

colonists with a new measure. The Quartering Act required the colonies to pay for the upkeep of British soldiers stationed in America. Long used to defending the colonies with local militia, the assemblies refused to vote funds for regular troops who would answer only to the royal governors. An angry Parliament responded with a new set of duties to pay troops and royal officials. Under the Townshend Acts, the assemblies would lose their control of colonial taxation and the power it gave them over the governors. When the assemblies protested, the governors closed more than half of them. Angry demonstrations swept the colonies. In the fall of 1768, the British army occupied Boston, America's largest port and the hotbed of colonial protest. The army forced a sullen peace on the city until March 5, 1770, when soldiers fired into an angry crowd, killing five men. The Boston Massacre touched off widespread rioting in Boston. Governor Thomas Hutchinson (1711–1780) prevented open warfare by clapping the soldiers in jail to await trial and then ordering the rest of the army out of the city.

After the Boston Massacre, cooler heads in Parliament repealed the Townshend Acts, leaving only a small duty on

Demanding "No taxation without representation," an angry crowd protests the Stamp Act of 1765.

In the infamous Boston Massacre, British soldiers
killed five patriots including Crispus Attucks,
a black dockworker. Although thousands of African
Americans—some free, some enslaved—joined the struggle
for American liberty, their sacrifices would go
unrewarded by the new nation.

tea. The colonial assemblies began meeting again, and there seemed hope that Britain and the colonies would settle their differences peaceably. But in 1773, Parliament revised the tea tax in another attempt to establish its right to control colonial trade. Boston again took the lead in organizing protests. When Governor Hutchinson refused to order three tea ships from the harbor, the Sons of Liberty boarded them and dumped their cargoes into the harbor in the famous Boston Tea Party. Parliament lost its temper and passed a set of harsh measures that threw the colonies into an uproar. What the Americans called the Intolerable Acts closed the port of Boston, stripped Massachusetts of its powers of self-government, imposed a stronger quartering act, limited the right of the colonies to try royal officials accused of crimes, and transferred all the lands north of the Ohio River to the Canadian province of Quebec.

The colonies rallied around Massachusetts. In late summer 1774, all of the colonies except Georgia sent representatives to the First Continental Congress in Philadelphia. The delegates agreed on a strong statement denying Parliament any right to impose taxes or to interfere in *any way* in the government of the colonies. To drive the message home, they approved a sweeping boycott of trade with Britain. While the Congress met, tensions rose in Massachusetts. General Thomas Gage (1721–1787), the new governor, brought five regiments of British soldiers to occupy Boston. Outside the city, the countryside was in

Thinly disguised as Indians,
Sons of Liberty empty
tea chests into the harbor
during the Boston Tea Party.

open rebellion. Minutemen companies drilled on village greens, their men pledging to meet a threat from British troops at a minute's notice. When Gage closed the Massachusetts assembly, its members met elsewhere as the Provincial Congress. They voted money for weapons, elected a war council, and sent messages to Rhode Island, Connecticut, and New Hampshire suggesting the formation of a New England army.

In Parliament, America's friends argued for fair treatment of the colonies, but the majority backed Prime Minister Lord Frederick North (1732–1792) and his harsh measures. North sent a message to Boston ordering General Gage to crush the rebellion in Massachusetts. On the night of April 18, 1775, 700 British soldiers set out for Lexington and nearby Concord to seize colonial arms and the patriot leaders John Hancock (1737–1793) and Samuel Adams. American spies sent word to William Dawes and Paul Revere (1735–1818), who rode into the countryside to spread the alarm. The news that the British were coming brought the Lexington militia hurrying to the village green at midnight. They waited through the long, cold hours at Buckman's Tavern and nearby houses. At 4:30 A.M., the rattle of the company drum brought them running onto the green. They formed awkward ranks under the orders of Captain John Parker. Down the road to the southeast came the steady tramp of marching men, then scarlet-clad soldiers swung into view in the first light of a new day.

The British advance guard of 350 light infantrymen shifted smoothly into attack formation to face the minutemen. The British commander rode forward and shouted, "Lay down your arms, you . . . rebels, and disperse." Parker hesitated and then gave the order for the minutemen to leave the field. He did not, however, tell them to leave their muskets behind. With the British officers shouting and the Americans hurrying away, someone fired a single shot. The British lines immediately opened fire, killing Parker and seven other minutemen. The surviving Americans fired a few wild shots and fled.

As the powder smoke drifted away, no one could tell who had fired the first shot of the American Revolution. History would call it "the shot heard round the world" and date the beginning of a new age from that dawn on Lexington Green.

Top: "The British are coming!" Paul Revere awakens a sleeping village on the night of April 18, 1775.

Bottom: With the "shot heard round the world" still echoing across Lexington Green, British troops open fire, killing eight minutemen and igniting the American Revolution.

Bidding a hasty farewell to their families,
Concord minutemen rush to defend their town.
Throughout the war, the work of running farms
and shops often fell to women and children.

TWO

WAR FOR INDEPENDENCE

THE CLASH on Lexington Green opened a long day of fighting. The British marched on to Concord with drums beating and fifes shrilling. Knots of minutemen hurried across the fields to get ahead of them. At the bridge on the far side of Concord, a sharp fight left three Americans and a dozen redcoats dead or wounded. Awakening to the danger gathering around them, the British began the 16-mile (26-km) return march to Boston. A mile east of Concord, a blast of musket fire tore into the column. The Americans fired from the cover of walls, trees, barns, and houses. They were untrained, disorganized, and—contrary to myth—terrible shots, but they were very angry. The British column, reinforced by 1,000 more soldiers, pushed ahead step by step as some 4,000 Americans joined the fight. At nightfall the column staggered into the safety of Charlestown, across the harbor from Boston. The British had lost 73 killed, 174 wounded, and 26 missing, three times the number of American casualties.

Hard-riding messengers carried news of the fighting through the colonies. Fifteen thousand New Englanders surrounded Boston. General Artemas Ward, the aged chief of the Massachusetts militia, took command. In the city, General Gage had fewer than half as many men, but they were skilled and disciplined professionals. For two months it was a standoff.

On the night of June 16, Ward sent 1,000 men to build an earthen fort, called a redoubt, atop Breed's Hill on Charlestown Peninsula. Gage saw the danger at first light. If completed, the redoubt's cannons could drive the Royal Navy's warships from Boston harbor, leaving the British army to starve. He sent General William Howe (1729–1814) to drive the rebels from the hill. Following European custom, Howe's men attacked in tightly packed ranks. The Americans at the redoubt and along a fence extending to the north shore cut them down in long scarlet rows. The proud British soldiers re-formed their ranks and charged again. On the third attempt, they burst through a weak point between the redoubt and the fence. Out of ammunition, the Americans fought with musket butts and stones, then broke and ran. What history would call the Battle of Bunker Hill (the name of a higher hill nearby) cost the British over 1,000 dead and wounded; the Americans more than 400.

Their gunpowder exhausted,
American militiamen use musket
butts and stones against
British troops charging
Breed's Hill in what came
to be called the
Battle of Bunker Hill.

On July 2, General George Washington (1732–1799) arrived in the American camp with orders from the Continental Congress to take command of the army. A hero of the French and Indian War, the Virginia plantation owner was the colonies' most famous soldier. John Adams (1735–1826), a leading Massachusetts patriot, had shrewdly suggested Washington's appointment to rally southern support for what was so far a New England war. At forty-three, Washington was a tall, handsome, almost forbiddingly dignified man. Although often troubled by self-doubts, he was completely dedicated to the "glorious cause" of American liberty. He set about making soldiers of the raw militiamen. He worked day and night to train, feed, and equip the army. Often it took all his efforts just to keep the army from simply melting away. As harvesttime approached, many of the militiamen headed home to farms and families. To give Washington more dependable soldiers, Congress authorized the formation of Continental regiments of full-time soldiers. For the rest of the war, the Continentals made up the army's tough core as the citizen soldiers of the militia came and went with the seasons.

As the siege of Boston dragged through the fall and into the winter, two small American armies marched into Canada. On the last day of 1775, they made a desperate attack on the capital city of Quebec. They ran into a trap in the narrow streets and were shot to pieces, ending American dreams for the capture of Canada. The news from Quebec

Gentleman farmer and hero of the French and Indian War,
General George Washington takes command of the raw
American army outside Boston in July 1775.

gave little comfort to the British soldiers in Boston. Supplies were running short as Washington's little navy of a half-dozen ships picked off incoming vessels. General Howe, who had replaced Gage in the fall, cut rations and ordered vacant buildings torn down for firewood.

The dawn of March 4, 1776, brought an ugly surprise for Howe. Awakened by an aide, he stared south across the harbor to Dorchester Heights. The Americans had thrown up redoubts in the night and were busily hauling cannons onto the heights to shell the city. The American cannons were from Fort Ticonderoga in northeastern New York. The fort and its big guns had been captured by the colorful Vermont patriot Ethan Allen (1738–1789) shortly after the battle in Lexington. Washington's artillery chief, a massive former bookseller named Henry Knox, had loaded fifty-eight of the guns aboard sledges in November and brought them across the frozen wilderness to Boston in one of the great feats of the war. Now, in a single night, the Americans had made it impossible for the British to stay in Boston. Howe sent word to Washington that he would not burn the city if the British were allowed to leave in peace. Two weeks later, the British army sailed for Halifax, Nova Scotia.

After nearly a year of war, the colonies had yet to decide if they were fighting for independence or only for fair treatment within the British Empire. The Continental Congress tried to open the way to peace with the Olive Branch

After nearly a year under siege by the American army,
the British set sail from Boston on March 17, 1776.

Petition, but the king refused to hear it. Parliament passed the Prohibitory Act, shutting off all trade with the colonies and seizing all ships caught violating the ban. The British government began hiring thousands of German soldiers—called Hessians by the Americans—to add to an army intended to crush the rebellion. The mood in America swung in favor of independence. Tens of thousands of Americans were convinced by the words of the fiery patriot Thomas Paine (1737–1809). In his essay *Common Sense*, Paine argued that America no longer needed a king and that it was ridiculous for a distant island to govern "a continent." Backed by the growing enthusiasm of the people, Congress selected a committee to write a message to the king and the world. A young Virginian, Thomas Jefferson (1743–1826), composed the document in ringing phrases. Congress approved the Declaration of Independence on July 4, 1776. In the streets of Philadelphia, church bells rang and cannons boomed to celebrate the birth of a new nation.

It fell to George Washington and his soldiers to make the Declaration more than a piece of paper. Expecting a British attack on New York—then a city of 25,000 on the southern tip of Manhattan Island—Washington had moved his army of 19,000 to the city and nearby Long Island. General Howe landed an army of 32,000 men on Staten Island in the harbor. On August 27, Howe attacked the American positions on Long Island. Outnumbered and

A Philadelphia crowd listens to America's Declaration
of Independence outside the Pennsylvania State House
—ever after known as Independence Hall.

outmaneuvered, the Americans suffered a huge defeat. But Howe was slow to follow up, and Washington saved the army with a skillful night crossing to Manhattan. On September 12, Howe struck north of the city, scattering the militia guarding the shore and nearly trapping Washington's army again. The Americans made another hair-breadth escape. Four days later, the Americans won a small victory at Harlem Heights, but disasters came one on top of another after that. On November 16, the British captured Fort Washington on the Hudson, taking 2,400 prisoners and a mountain of weapons and supplies. Howe's aggressive second in command, Lord Charles Cornwallis (1738–1805), chased Washington across New Jersey. Starving and exhausted, the Americans crossed the Delaware River into Pennsylvania in early December, leaving no boats for the British to use.

Top: After a disastrous defeat at the Battle of Long Island, the Continental army makes a night escape to Manhattan Island.

Bottom: With the Revolution seemingly doomed, Washington crosses the Delaware River on Christmas Day 1776 for a desperate attack on the Hessian garrison at Trenton, New Jersey.

Philadelphia, the young nation's capital, lay only 30 miles (50 km) from the river. On the north shore, Cornwallis's 10,000 men waited for the river to freeze so that they could cross on the ice. Washington's 3,000 ragged soldiers waited on the south shore with little hope that they could keep the Revolution alive much longer. Washington himself wrote a nephew: "I think the game is pretty near up." Then General Howe made an astonishing decision. With victory nearly in his grasp, he ordered his troops into winter quarters in a string of posts from Trenton on the Delaware to New York City. Washington formed a desperate plan to save the Revolution. Late on Christmas Day, 1776, his army boarded boats to cross the Delaware. Lashed by wind and sleet, the men rowed through floating ice to the New Jersey shore. Ragged and shoeless, they left bloody footprints as they marched through the terrible night. Yet Washington's example and their own belief in the "glorious cause" kept them moving. At 8:00 A.M., the Americans roared into Trenton, overwhelming the unsuspecting Hessian garrison. At the cost of only four casualties, the Americans killed or wounded over 100 Hessians and took nearly 1,000 prisoners.

A few days later, the Americans fought a vicious draw with Cornwallis near Trenton. The Americans circled around Cornwallis's army in the night and pounced on three British regiments at Princeton, New Jersey, on the morning of January 3, 1777. Dodging Cornwallis yet

The Continental army's resounding victory at the Battle of Trenton saved the "glorious cause" of American independence.

again, Washington led his tired but triumphant soldiers into winter quarters at Morristown, New Jersey. In the darkest days of the war, Washington's army had won stunning victories at Trenton and Princeton. All through the colonies, hope burned bright again.

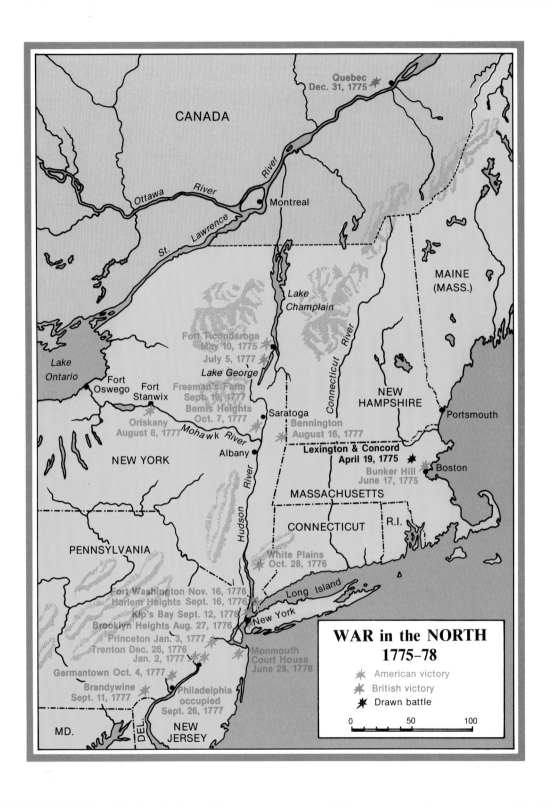

CANADA

Quebec
Dec. 31, 1775

Ottawa River

St. Lawrence River

Montreal

Lake Champlain

MAINE
(MASS.)

Lake Ontario

Fort Oswego

Fort Stanwix

Fort Ticonderoga
May 10, 1775
July 5, 1777

Lake George

Freeman's Farm
Sept. 19, 1777
Bemis Heights
Oct. 7, 1777

Oriskany
August 6, 1777

Mohawk River

Saratoga

Connecticut River

NEW
HAMPSHIRE

Portsmouth

Bennington
August 16, 1777

Albany

NEW YORK

Hudson River

Lexington & Concord
April 19, 1775

Bunker Hill
June 17, 1775

Boston

MASSACHUSETTS

CONNECTICUT

R.I.

PENNSYLVANIA

White Plains
Oct. 28, 1776

Fort Washington Nov. 16, 1776
Harlem Heights Sept. 16, 1776
Kip's Bay Sept. 12, 1776
Brooklyn Heights Aug. 27, 1776
Princeton Jan. 3, 1777
Trenton Dec. 26, 1776
Jan. 2, 1777

Germantown Oct. 4, 1777

Brandywine
Sept. 11, 1777

Philadelphia
occupied
Sept. 26, 1777

Long Island

New York

Monmouth
Court House
June 28, 1778

MD.

DEL.

NEW
JERSEY

**WAR in the NORTH
1775–78**

✳ American victory

✳ British victory

✳ Drawn battle

0   50   100

YEARS OF TRIAL

W A S H I N G T O N rebuilt his army at Morristown in the early months of 1777. Through the summer he maneuvered carefully in New Jersey, waiting for Howe to make the next move. Meanwhile, an American army in upstate New York prepared to meet a British invasion from Canada. The British plan was the creation of General John Burgoyne (1722–1792). He proposed bringing a powerful army south over Lake Champlain to meet another British force coming east from Lake Ontario along the Mohawk Valley. At the same time, Howe would bring his army up the Hudson River from New York City. Burgoyne's march would bring the Iroquois Indians, who had long resented the trespassing of American settlers, into the war on the British side. The meeting with Howe would cut off New England from the rest of the colonies and knock New York out of the war.

Burgoyne's invasion began well. His army of 8,300 men

reached Fort Ticonderoga near the southern end of Lake Champlain on July 1. The Americans abandoned the fort and fled in boats. Burgoyne chased them to Skenesboro, Vermont, where the Americans burned their boats and escaped into the forest. Burgoyne faced a march of 23 miles (37 km) along a rough road through heavy woods to Fort Edward on the Hudson. Too proud to fall back a few miles to an easy water route through Lake George, Burgoyne ordered his army forward. American woodsmen cut down trees and diverted streams to block the road, and it took the British three painful weeks to reach the Hudson.

General Horatio Gates (1728–1806) used the delay to gather a large American army to block Burgoyne's way south. To the west, American troops in the Mohawk Valley turned back the small British army coming from Lake Ontario. To the east, New Hampshire militia pounced on one of Burgoyne's raiding parties, killing or capturing 900 Hessians at Bennington, Vermont. Meanwhile, General Howe received conflicting instructions from Britain and decided to attack Philadelphia rather than march up the Hudson to meet Burgoyne.

Burgoyne pushed ahead until he collided with Gates north of Albany. At the Battle of Freeman's Farm on September 19, Gates's second in command, the brilliant and daring Benedict Arnold (1741–1801), led an American attack that shattered the British advance and almost cut Burgoyne's army in two. But Gates failed to send in more troops at the critical moment. After the battle, the two generals argued, and Gates relieved Arnold of further duty.

Still expecting a British move north from New York City, Burgoyne settled in to wait for help. By October 7, the American army had almost doubled in size, and Burgoyne could wait no longer. He launched a desperate attempt to break through Gates's army in the Battle of Bemis Heights. Watching Gates miss another chance for a great victory, Arnold leaped on his horse and dashed into the fighting. He led two wild assaults on the British center,

Led by the daring General Benedict Arnold,
American troops smash through the British lines at
the Battle of Bemis Heights, New York.

General John Burgoyne surrenders his soldiers to General
Horatio Gates at Saratoga, New York, on October 17, 1777.

broke through, and sent Burgoyne's troops tumbling back.
The British retreated to the heights of Saratoga on the
Hudson. Surrounded, Burgoyne surrendered his remaining
6,000 men on October 17, 1777. Congress showered the
bumbling Gates with praise but ignored Arnold. Three
years later, an embittered Arnold would sell out to the
British and become the most infamous traitor in American
history.

News of Burgoyne's surrender at Saratoga gave heart to
Washington's army in Pennsylvania, where it had suffered

another string of discouraging defeats. The army had moved south from New Jersey in late July to block Howe's move on Philadelphia. Howe's army arrived by ship from New York City, landing at the head of Chesapeake Bay, 50 miles (80 km) from the nation's capital. Washington made his stand along Brandywine Creek halfway between the bay and Philadelphia. On September 11, Howe attacked and gave the Americans a thorough thumping. But Washington's army shook off the defeat and again blocked Howe's way. For two weeks the armies maneuvered. Tired of the game, Howe tricked Washington into a move west, then circled back to enter Philadelphia unopposed on September 26.

To Howe's disgust, the American cause did not crumble with the loss of Philadelphia. The Continental Congress carried on its work in another city—it would move nine times in its lifetime—while the villages and farms beyond British control continued to man and feed the Continental army. On October 4, Washington surprised Howe's camp at Germantown, outside Philadelphia. For a short time, it looked as if the Americans would win the greatest victory of the war. Then Howe rallied his splendidly disciplined troops and led them in a strong counterattack. Running short of ammunition, the Americans had to retreat yet again.

Washington's army took up winter quarters on a windy plateau 18 miles (29 km) northwest of Philadelphia.

Washington's attack on General Howe's camp at Germantown, Pennsylvania, breaks against the stout walls of Chew House.

Named for an abandoned iron furnace nearby, Valley Forge became the scene of terrible suffering in the winter of 1777–78. The soldiers hung on through months of bitter cold and short rations. Onto this bleak landscape strode a stocky, red-faced German who would give the soldiers a new sense of pride. Baron Friedrich von Steuben (1730–1794) was a former Prussian army officer and Washington's new inspector general of training. Using both firmness and humor, Steuben taught the Continental army to maneuver and fight with the speed and discipline of a European army.

Great news for the American cause came from France in the spring of 1778. In 1776 Congress had sent the world-famous scientist, writer, philosopher, and diplomat Benjamin Franklin (1706–1790) to Paris to win French aid for the Revolution. Playing on France's desire to weaken the British Empire, he had obtained money and supplies. But Franklin wanted more than gold and gunpowder; he wanted French soldiers and—most important of all—the help of the French navy. The powerful British navy controlled the coast of America, landing raiders and choking off American shipping. With French help, the Americans could even the odds ashore and at sea. Dr. Franklin used the victory at Saratoga and the gallant effort at Germantown to persuade the French government to join the war on the side of America.

The French declaration of war in June 1778 changed the

Top: A shivering sentry
waits for his relief
during the terrible
winter at Valley Forge.

Bottom: Beaver hat warming
his balding head,
Benjamin Franklin strolls
the streets of Paris
with his grandsons.
Using cunning, patience,
and wit, Franklin convinced
the French government to
assist the Revolution.

conflict into a struggle between two great empires fighting in North America, Europe, and the Far East. Needing troops to guard rich islands in the Caribbean, the British government ordered General Henry Clinton (1738–1795), who had replaced Howe, to abandon Philadelphia. The army started the march to New York City with the redcoats guarding a train of supply wagons 12 miles (19 km) long. The newly confident Continental army struck the British rear guard at Monmouth Court House, New Jersey. Washington's second in command, General Charles Lee—a boastful and vain professional soldier—botched the attack, ordering a retreat before most of the American soldiers had even fired a shot. Washington arrived, fired Lee on the spot, and rallied the troops. The Americans formed a line and withstood repeated charges by Clinton's best soldiers. In the night, the British army slipped away. By dawn it was out of reach. A disappointed Washington led his army to White Plains, near New York City.

For the next three years, Washington and his men would guard against a British move from the city. The Continentals were bored, ill-equipped, poorly fed, and rarely paid. Only Washington's commanding presence kept the army together. Time and again Washington tried to arrange a joint effort by French and American forces, but cooperation proved difficult. Twice a French fleet arrived, only to sail away on other missions before anything meaningful could be accomplished.

Setting aside the pitcher of water she had been carrying
to thirsty soldiers, Mary McCauley—later celebrated as
Molly Pitcher—takes the place of her wounded husband at
the Battle of Monmouth Court House.

John Paul Jones's *Bonhomme Richard* pounds the British
frigate *Serapis* into surrender on September 23, 1779.

While Washington's army waited for its chance, fighting continued elsewhere. British ships landed raiders to burn coastal towns. American warships and privateers—armed merchant vessels authorized to hunt British merchant ships—played cat and mouse with the Royal Navy. The great American seaman John Paul Jones (1747–1792) twice sailed around the British Isles, picking off merchant ships and raiding the coast. On September 23, 1779, his ship *Bonhomme Richard* pounded the British frigate *Serapis* into surrender in the most famous American naval victory of the war.

On the New York and Pennsylvania frontiers, American settlers fought Britain's Iroquois allies. Like most whites of his day, Washington had little sympathy for the Native Americans. Following Washington's harsh orders, General John Sullivan burned some forty Iroquois villages and tens of thousands of bushels of food in the summer of 1779. The Iroquois never recovered.

Farther west, Colonel George Rogers Clark (1752–1818) captured the key outpost of Vincennes in today's Indiana, stalemating the British threat in the Ohio Valley. After the war, Clark's daring exploits would give the Americans claim to the Old Northwest, a vast area that would become the states of Ohio, Indiana, Illinois, Michigan, Wisconsin, and part of Minnesota. But the day when peace negotiators could draw boundaries on maps was yet far away. A war had to be won—or lost.

CLIMAX IN THE SOUTH

BY THE autumn of 1778, the war had become a deadlock. Too weak to win and too stubborn to quit, the Americans hung onto their dream of independence. Needing a new plan to win the war, the frustrated British decided to invade the southern colonies. The American cause was weakest in Georgia and the Carolinas, where many of the people remained loyal to the king. A successful invasion of the South could rally thousands of Loyalists to the king's army. The army could then march north into Virginia, the richest of the thirteen colonies, to deliver a knockout blow to the Revolution.

General Clinton directed the plan from his headquarters in New York City. In the last week of 1778, a British army captured Savannah, Georgia. The following spring it moved on Charleston, South Carolina, the only large city in the South. The Americans drove the British off and tried to recapture Savannah in the summer of 1779. A French

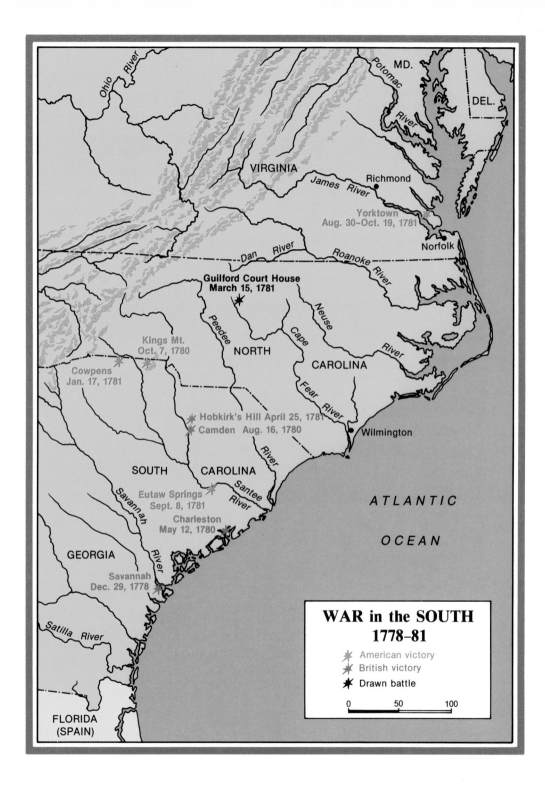

MD.

DEL.

Ohio River

Potomac River

VIRGINIA

James River   Richmond

Yorktown
Aug. 30–Oct. 19, 1781

Norfolk

Dan River   *Roanoke River*

**Guilford Court House
March 15, 1781**

Kings Mt.
Oct. 7, 1780

Peedee River

NORTH

Neuse River

Cape Fear River

CAROLINA

Cowpens
Jan. 17, 1781

Hobkirk's Hill April 25, 1781
Camden Aug. 16, 1780

Wilmington

SOUTH   CAROLINA

Santee River

Savannah River

Eutaw Springs
Sept. 8, 1781

ATLANTIC

OCEAN

Charleston
May 12, 1780

GEORGIA

Savannah
Dec. 29, 1778

Satilla River

FLORIDA
(SPAIN)

WAR in the SOUTH
1778–81

✳ American victory
✳ British victory
✳ Drawn battle

0   50   100

Furious fire from American forts drives off British warships
attacking Charleston, South Carolina. The British tried to capture
Charleston twice before finally succeeding in 1780.

fleet arrived to help, but again cooperation fell apart, and
the Americans suffered a painful defeat. In the spring of
1780, Clinton sailed south with a large army to capture
Charleston. Scores of British cannons shelled the city as
Clinton's men dug trenches toward the American fortifications. General Benjamin Lincoln's American soldiers
fought back with everything they had. Finally, with ammunition running short and the city's civilians cowering under

a rain of British shells, Lincoln surrendered. In the worst defeat yet for the American army, the British took 3,400 prisoners and 343 cannons. General Clinton returned to New York City, leaving his second in command, Lord Charles Cornwallis, to build a string of bases across South Carolina.

The loss of Charleston staggered the American cause. The long years of war had ravaged the country's economy. The money printed by the Continental Congress had almost no value left, and Congress was having more and more difficulty borrowing money abroad to pay for the war. The colonies bickered, behaving more like thirteen individual countries than one nation fighting for independence. Not since the early winter of 1776 had the Revolution seemed so close to collapse.

In the South Carolina countryside, small patriot bands led by Thomas Sumter, Andrew Pickens, and Francis Marion—the famed Swamp Fox—fought a nasty, no-holds-barred war against the British and the Loyalists. Washington longed to march his army south, but he could not leave the middle colonies open to an invasion by Clinton's powerful army in New York City. Washington decided to send the Baron Johann DeKalb (1721–1780)—a remarkable German soldier of fortune—and 1,400 Continentals to rally American militia for an attack on Cornwallis's base at Camden, South Carolina. Without consulting Washington, Congress demoted DeKalb and put Horatio Gates—the "hero of Saratoga"—in command. Gates discarded DeKalb's carefully laid plans and nearly starved the army to death on the march to Camden. On the morning of August 16, 1780, the exhausted Americans met Cornwallis's seasoned and rested veterans. The British charged, their long rows of bayonets glinting. At the fearsome sight, the American militia broke and ran. Gates leaped on the army's fastest horse and fled. DeKalb's Continentals stood their ground, fighting like demons until a cavalry charge shattered their ranks. Wounded eleven times, DeKalb died two days later.

Washington fired Gates, replacing him with Major General Nathanael Greene (1742–1786), one of the unsung heroes of the American Revolution. A Rhode Island merchant, Greene had spent his personal fortune in the American cause. He had served Washington skillfully as a field commander, then taken over the quartermaster department during the terrible winter at Valley Forge. Somehow he had managed to find the supplies to keep the army alive. Delighted to leave paperwork behind at last, Greene hurried south. The disaster at Camden had left the southern army with only 1,500 men. Until he rebuilt the battered army, he could not take on Cornwallis in a stand-up fight, but he could drive the British crazy with sudden strikes and fast getaways. Greene's cavalry rode into the South Carolina countryside to make war on the Loyalists. General Daniel Morgan (1736–1802), Greene's superb second in command, took 600 Continentals west to rally militia and to threaten the British outpost at the oddly named town of Ninety-Six.

Cornwallis took the bait. He had already suffered one disaster in western South Carolina, when militia had slaughtered a large force of Loyalists at King's Mountain in October, and he was not about to let Morgan run wild in the area. Leaving part of his army to watch Greene's base at Cheraw, South Carolina, he sent his feared cavalry chieftain, Colonel Banastre Tarleton (1754–1833), after Morgan. Cornwallis maneuvered with the remainder of the army to cut off Morgan's line of escape.

Morgan was delighted with the prospect of fighting the ruthless Tarleton. The bearlike Morgan understood militiamen and knew how to make the inexperienced men fight. North of Ninety-Six, he laid a trap on a plain called Cowpens. Tarleton's 1,100 cavalry and infantry arrived on the morning of January 17, 1781, to find Morgan's men drawn up in three widely spaced lines. As Tarleton's men attacked, each American line delivered a punishing fire, then withdrew. When the third line disappeared over a hill, Tarleton thought the Americans were running and ordered

Colonel William Washington crosses swords with the hated British cavalry chieftain Banastre Tarleton at the Battle of Cowpens on January 17, 1781.

an all-out pursuit. His men cheered, broke ranks, and charged over the hill in a mob. The Americans were waiting for them along a second lower hill. A blast of musket fire tore into the British. The Continentals charged with bayonets. The British threw down their weapons and begged for mercy. Only Tarleton and a few cavalry escaped.

With Cornwallis in hot pursuit, Morgan raced north to join the rest of Greene's army already withdrawing into North Carolina. Greene had a simple but brilliant plan. His army was still too weak to fight Cornwallis's, but it could march the British to death in a race for the safety of Virginia on the far side of the wide, deep Dan River. The two parts of Greene's army joined at Guilford Court House, North Carolina, then slogged north in a steady winter rain. The British trudged doggedly behind, trying to make up the few miles separating the armies. On February 10, a decoy force led the British to the west as Greene's army began the final sprint for the Dan. For four grueling days, the decoy force stayed barely ahead of the British. In sixteen hours it covered the last 40 miles (65 km) to the river. Only minutes ahead of the British, the Americans boarded the last boats and hauled for the north shore.

On the south shore of the Dan, Cornwallis's army lay exhausted, its ranks drained by sickness and desertion, its nearest supply base 230 miles (370 km) to the south. Greene rested his army in friendly Virginia, then recrossed the river on February 23. He camped at Guilford Court House, inviting a fight. Cornwallis took the challenge on March 15. Greene met the attack with a plan much like Morgan's at Cowpens. Again each American line fired a few punishing volleys, then withdrew with only light losses. At the end of the afternoon, Greene's army marched coolly away, leaving British officers to claim victory on a field littered with redcoat dead. In reality, Greene had marched and bled the British army nearly to death. The campaign had cost Cornwallis 2,600 of his 4,000 men. Unable to win in the Carolinas, Cornwallis marched north to try his luck in Virginia.

Cornwallis took command of the British army raiding along the James River in Virginia, but could not lure into a major battle the small American army under the young Marquis de Lafayette (1757–1834), a gallant French volunteer. Frustrated again, Cornwallis withdrew to Yorktown on Chesapeake Bay to wait for further orders from Clinton in New York City.

Washington's army was still camped near New York. The Comte de Rochambeau (1725–1807) had arrived with 5,000 French regulars, and Washington suggested an attack on the city. Rochambeau discouraged the idea, arguing that the British defenses were too strong. The two generals were still debating the issue when a letter arrived that changed the course of the war. Admiral the Comte de Grasse (1722–1788) wrote that he was bringing the

French Caribbean fleet to Chesapeake Bay at the end of August and departing in mid-October. In the weeks between, he would be happy to cooperate with the Americans.

Washington grabbed the chance. With the country's economy in a shambles, the Revolution might not survive another winter. He would leave New York City unguarded and risk everything for a great victory at Yorktown. He sent orders instructing Lafayette to watch Cornwallis closely, then set about getting the army ready to move. On August 21, carefully disguising their departure, the American and French troops marched south. On September 2, the army paraded through the streets of Philadelphia on its way to the coast to board transports for the trip down the Chesapeake. Washington and Rochambeau waited anxiously for news of the French fleet. If the British fleet beat de Grasse to the Chesapeake, the whole gigantic campaign would come to nothing. On September 4, Rochambeau rode into the American camp to find Washington, usually the most restrained of men, "waving his hat at me with . . . the greatest joy." De Grasse had arrived at the Chesapeake ahead of the British fleet; Cornwallis was trapped.

On September 5, de Grasse's ships drove off the British fleet trying to enter the bay, sealing Cornwallis's fate. The French and the American troops began arriving at Yorktown. Surrounding the town, they started digging siege trenches on October 6. Day after day the trenches lengthened, bringing the cannons closer and closer to the town

Generals Rochambeau and Washington
watch as the British defenses
at Yorktown, Virginia, crumble
under the fire of French
and American cannons.

already smoking under constant shelling. A night attack on October 14 cleared two British redoubts and brought the American and French cannons within 300 yards (275 m) of the town's fortifications. The end was near. On the morning of October 17, the French and the Americans opened fire with all their guns. As the British fortifications crumbled and the proud redcoats huddled in the smoke and dust, Cornwallis called for a truce. On October 19, 1781, British soldiers, numbering 8,087, marched out of Yorktown to lay down their arms.

The American victory at Yorktown broke the will of the British government to continue the war. In Paris, peace talks began in April 1782, and the final treaty was signed on September 3, 1783. Eight and a half years after the "shot heard round the world" rang out on Lexington Green, Americans became a free and independent people.

Lord Charles Cornwallis surrenders to General George Washington at Yorktown, Virginia. The great American victory forced the British government to call for peace.

THE FLINTLOCK MUSKET

BOTH SIDES in the American Revolution fought with flintlock muskets. A soldier carried paper-wrapped ammunition in a cartridge pouch slung at his side. To load his musket, he tore the end of a cartridge with his teeth and sprinkled gunpowder into the pan of the firing mechanism, where it would be set off by a spark when the piece of flint on the hammer struck the steel latch covering the pan. He then pushed the rest of the cartridge into the open end of the barrel and jammed the powder and bullet down with a long steel rod called a ramrod. Despite the lengthy procedure, an expert could fire three or four shots a minute.

The standard British Brown Bess musket was some 5 feet (1.5 m) long, weighed 10 pounds (4.5 kg), and fired a lead ball of more than an ounce (28 g). Although accurate only to about 75 yards (67.5 m), it was a particularly

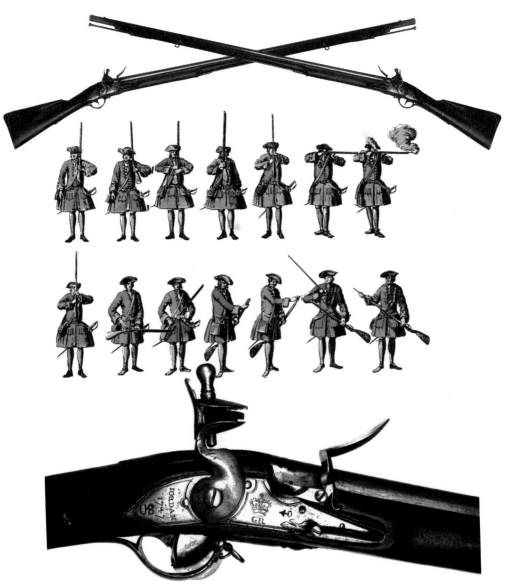

deadly weapon in the hands of infantrymen firing in tight
ranks. After two or three volleys, the ranks usually charged
to finish the battle with the 21-inch (54-cm) bayonets fixed
to the end of their muskets.

SUGGESTED READING

Carter, Alden R. *Colonies in Revolt*. New York: Franklin Watts, 1988.

_____. *Darkest Hours*. New York: Franklin Watts, 1988.

_____. *At the Forge of Liberty*. New York: Franklin Watts, 1988.

_____. *Birth of the Republic*. New York: Franklin Watts, 1988.

Lancaster, Bruce. *The American Heritage Book of the American Revolution*. New York: American Heritage, 1971.

Lengyel, Cornel. *The Declaration of Independence*. New York: Grosset and Dunlap, 1968.

McDowell, Bart. *The Revolutionary War*. Washington, D.C.: National Geographic Society, 1967.

Middlekauff, Robert. *The Glorious Cause*. New York: Oxford University Press, 1982.

Sanderlin, George. *1776: Journals of American Independence*. New York: Harper and Row, 1968.

Ward, Christopher. *The War of the Revolution*. New York: Macmillan, 1952.

Wright, Esmond. *The Fire of Liberty*. New York: St. Martin's Press, 1983.

INDEX

Adams, John, 22
Adams, Samuel, 9, 15
Allen, Ethan, 24
American Revolution
　　(1775–1783):
　　Boston, siege of, 22–
　　　　24
　　British campaign in
　　　　the South, 45–54
　　British invasion from
　　　　Canada, 33–36
　　Bunker Hill, battle of,
　　　　20
　　Declaration of
　　　　Independence, 26
　　French declaration of
　　　　war, 39–41
　　Lexington and
　　　　Concord, battles of,
　　　　7, 15–17, 19–20
　　Long Island, battle of,
　　　　26–28
　　Philadelphia, loss of,
　　　　36–37

　　prelude to, 7–17
　　Trenton and Princeton,
　　　　victories at, 30–31
　　Valley Forge, 37–39
　　Yorktown, victory at,
　　　　54–57
Arnold, Benedict, 34–36

Bonhomme Richard, 44
Boston, Massachusetts,
　　siege of, 22–24
Boston Massacre, 11
Boston Tea Party, 13
British campaign in the
　　South, 45–54
Bunker Hill, battle of, 20
Burgoyne, General John,
　　33–36

Camden, South Carolina,
　　battle of, 48
Charleston, South
　　Carolina, capture of,
　　45–48

Clark, Colonel George
    Rogers, 44
Clinton, General Henry,
    41, 45, 47–48
Common Sense (Paine),
    26
Concord, Massachusetts,
    battle of, 19–20
Continental Congress, 13,
    22, 24–26, 37, 48
Cornwallis, Lord Charles,
    28, 30, 48, 49, 50, 53,
    57
Cowpens, South Carolina,
    battle of, 50–52

Dawes, William, 15
Declaration of
    Independence, 26
De Grasse, Admiral the
    Comte, 53–54
DeKalb, Baron Johann,
    48–49

Flintlock muskets, 58–
    59
Franklin, Benjamin, 39
French declaration of war,
    39–41

Gage, General Thomas,
    13–14, 20, 24
Gates, General Horatio,
    34–35, 49
Greene, Major General
    Nathanael, 49, 52–53
Guilford Court House,
    North Carolina, battle
    of, 53

Hancock, John, 15
Howe, General William,
    20, 24, 26–27, 30, 34,
    37
Hutchinson, Thomas, 11, 13

Iroquois Indians, 33, 44

Jefferson, Thomas, 26
Jones, John Paul, 44

Knox, Henry, 24

Lafayette, Marquis de, 53,
    54
Lee, General Charles,
    41
Lexington, Massachusetts,
    battle of, 7, 15–17

ABOUT THE AUTHOR

ALDEN R. CARTER is a versatile writer for children and young adults. He has written nonfiction books on electronics, supercomputers, radio, Illinois, Shoshoni Indians, the People's Republic of China, the Alamo, the Battle of Gettysburg, the Colonial Wars, the War of 1812, the Mexican War, the Civil War, the Spanish-American War, and four books on the American Revolution: *Colonies in Revolt, Darkest Hours, At the Forge of Liberty*, and *Birth of the Republic*. His novels *Growing Season* (1984), *Wart, Son of Toad* (1985), *Sheila's Dying* (1987), and *Up Country* (1989) were named to the American Library Association's annual lists of Best Books for Young Adults. His fifth novel, *RoboDad*, was honored as Best Children's Fiction Book of 1990 by the Society of Midland Authors. Mr. Carter lives with his wife, Carol, and their children, Brian Patrick and Siri Morgan, in Marshfield, Wisconsin.